PROFIT FROM POSSIBILITIES

A Look At The World In 2050

A Report By
Adrian Kennedy

PROFIT FROM POSSIBILITIES

A Look At The World In 2050

A Report By Adrian Kennedy

Published by Xscape Publishing in the United States (the "Publisher")

History Doesn't Repeat It Rhymes.

Many lives will be destroyed.

They won't be destroyed by any physical threat. They will be destroyed due to the lack of preparation and planning. I want you to be prepared.

Understand that this report is not an attempt to predict or forecast the future. I'm not smart enough to try to do that. However, I am dumb enough to simply study history, follow trends and pay attention to events and trends that may occur in the future. This report looks at events that are currently occurring or have a possibility of occurring within a certain level of probability.

The reason why I'm writing this guide is because I have gained a unique perspective from working for governments and the private sector across industries in the United States and Australia. In addition to this work, I've also worked for Clients and with Customers around the world.

This guide comes from a place of healthy paranoia and skepticism that forces me to be forward looking. This forward-looking approach to life has led to me to thrive from events such as the housing collapse in 2006 and the Global Financial Crisis in 2008. I was able to profit from these events by studying history, paying attention to current trends and events and positioning myself to capitalize on these possibilities if they did happen and if they didn't happen, I would still be in a great position due to me adding to my knowledge, experience, skill toolbox and assets.

But it's really no fun if you and your loved ones, friends and associates are the only ones in your circle whose house doesn't burn down when the entire world is on fire all around you.

I've decided that I wouldn't be selfish like I was in the past and decided to share this information with those who are willing to receive it, learn from it and use it to drive them to action.

This report was created to help others profit from potential outcomes while hopefully minimizing their losses in financially negative situations. The information shared in the report is not just random information but builds on things I'm actually involved in and preparing for myself in one way or another.

My goal in this report is to use research and analysis to help create and grow multi-generation wealth as we experience the only constant in life...

Change.

In this case, historic change.

I'm Talking To You

Yes, this report is written specifically for you.

I write for people who take action.

This report is written for people who are willing to be honest with themselves and simply Pay Attention to their surroundings. People who will verify for themselves whether the information I am sharing with them is true. Don't take anything at face value. Question everything.

This report is for people who may not have any savings, may not have any assets, may not have finished high school and have never considered starting a business. And if you do have savings, degrees, a business or whatever then that's great. It really doesn't matter because the information I will share is presented in a format that anyone can understand and apply.

I will give you the process, tools, resources and systems that will help prevent you from being your own worst enemy.

Unlearn

You've been lied to.

You will be lied to again. And you won't be the only one that will be lied to.

The worst thing about the lies you will be told is that the people telling the lies will truly believe that they are telling you the truth.

Conventional wisdom is often wrong. The belief systems that most people are wrong about will only lead to an average life.

I shine light on some of this disinformation and misinformation in an effort to help others benefit from objective truths. Painful truths. Truths that admit that human nature is often unavoidable. Truths that acknowledge that many of us are still animals driven by our base instincts. Instincts that arise from our lower reptilian instincts as opposed to our Paleomammalian brain that drives our consumptions, relationships and parenting behaviors or our higher level Neomammalian brain that drives our communication, planning and perception.

However, if we are aware of how certain external stimulus is meant to appeal to our base instincts, we can gain more control over our lives. We can use habits and behaviors that are interpreted to be "bad" to our benefit if you put the right processes and systems in place.

Let's talk about a few of these lies people are told that should go away and what they should be.

Buy a house because it's your biggest asset. This should be to buy real estate that generates income as an asset for yourself. Living in a house is a liability. The rule is that an asset puts more money in your pocket every month and year than it takes out.

Do what you love. This should be do what makes money. Love may keep families and communities together, but it doesn't pay bills. So, it's important to find what others are willing to pay you for either as an employee or business owner then provide them with that product or service.

Save money. This should be to make more money. Unless the money is being put into motion to earn more money, you will never save your way into wealth unless you are already generating a high income as a person or business and the net income after your expenses allows you to save multiples of your monthly expenses every month.

Save for retirement. This should be to find more ways to earn money before and during retirement (if you plan to retire at all). I personally believe that "saving for retirement" is a dream sold to keep people chasing an unachievable goal so the system can keep extracting work from them for life. But I'm just paranoid.

I personally believe in lifestyle design and financial independence as the goals people should achieve, but here is some data about saving for retirement.

According to the World Bank, the average life expectancy in the US in 2016 was nearly 80 years old.

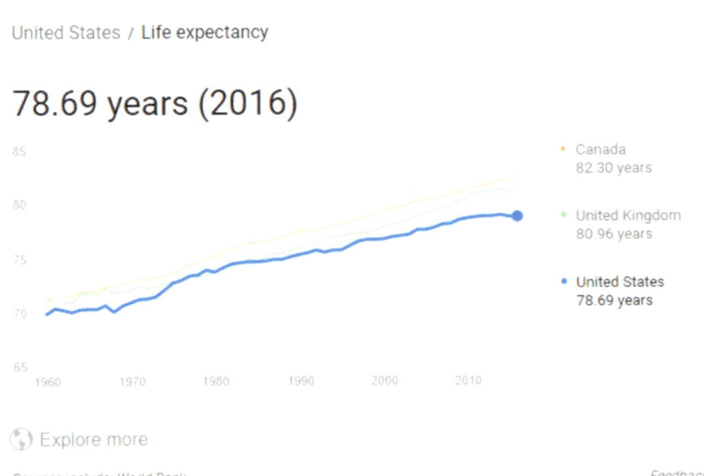

According to the Economic Policy Institute, most people won't have enough retirement savings by the time they reach retirement age and people who were working age (32-61) in 2013 had less than $200,000 on average.

And these numbers don't account for the number of people who are living beyond the average life expectancy of 80 years old. Retirement savings plans are great in theory but considering that many people are in retirement for 20-40 years, they may give people false hope when there are mathematical impossibilities.

Retirement savings have stagnated in the new millennium
Mean retirement account savings of families by age, 1989–2013 (2013 dollars)

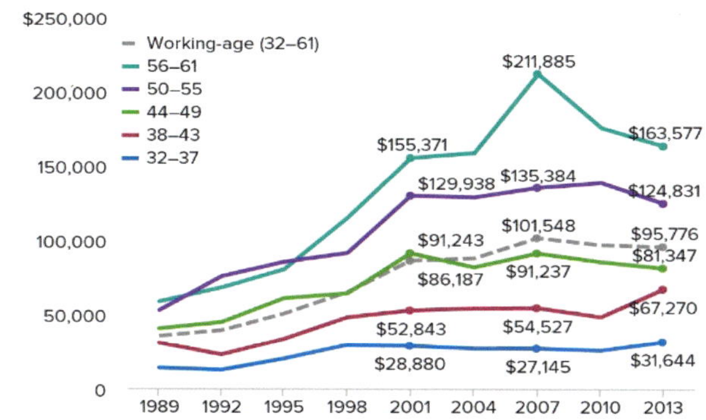

Note: Retirement account savings include 401(k)s, IRAs, and Keogh plans.
Source: EPI analysis of Survey of Consumer Finance data, 2013.

Having gone through the numbers, the only solution to the problems this situation will create is for people to learn to earn more.

Network equals Net Worth. This should be Community equals Net Worth.

For too long many have interpreted networking as telling lots of people about their degree, career or what product or service they have to offer. This is the selfish way of growing a career or business. If you truly want to increase your net worth, focus on growing your community.

Find a good job. This should be to find a good career that helps you grow and advance. I've had a lot of jobs in my life and all of them had their issues. It wasn't until I shifted my mindset away from jobs and towards career paths that I found fulfillment.

A career path, unlike a job, is not a destination but is a journey with several possible exits that you can choose to stop at along your way towards professional growth.

Pay yourself first. This should be to pay yourself first and help others to pay themselves first. This payment to yourself and others may be money, but it doesn't always have to be.

Having been mentored by several people and having mentored people myself, paying yourself and others can be as simple as educating yourself before you teach others. Because while paying yourself first may add to your nest egg, the information and experience gained from learning how to pay yourself first are priceless. Paying this information forward to others so they can do the same can carry a lot of value in even when no money changes hands.

Education as the goal to be praised should be replaced with real-world experience being praised.

You are Your Own Company

Don't ever think that just because you have a job or career that you aren't a business owner. You are just as responsible for managing your life as if it was a business as anyone else.

The following information is meant for people who have jobs but want to grow in the coming years and decades.

The following sections related to Career Growth and Education are based on observations of current trends and other topics that will be discussed later in the report.

Traditional Educational Institutions Are Dying

Due to politics, watered-down fields of study, extravagant costs and market saturation of degrees of all levels, the traditional university model is dying. I'm working to help that death happen sooner by providing information directly to people at a fraction of what it would cost in a university.

The only schools that will retain their value are top tier schools that are better for the people networks they provide access to, especially top STEM schools and trade specific schools.

In my view, STEM will continue to offer the best return on investment when it comes to education. However, STEM education often doesn't require traditional schooling for many fields due to experience being treated as attaining varying levels of schooling.

When it comes to non-STEM fields, the Trades will continue to see growth regardless of economic conditions. Especially traditional trades like Electricians, Plumbers and Healthcare professions will continue to grow.

How value in education is shifting away from the traditional university model for non-STEM degrees and toward professional certifications and boot camps?

The end of this newsletter contains tables of resources.

No One Will Pay You Better Than You Can Pay Yourself

There is nothing wrong with having a 9-5 job or working a trade. The reality is that any work that allows you to provide for yourself and your loved one should be considered a "good job."

But a job will merely get you from point A to point B and may not provide the extra financial resources and time that will allow you to pursue your passions and have more control over your time.

To gain more money and time, you have to grow your own business and investments. A job is great, but you can't pass down a job.

The next few sections focus on trends I've observed that may or may not be relevant to growing your business but are observations that are worth noting.

My Political Stance Is Leave Me and My Money Alone

I've worked two Presidential Elections and have been involved in politics at various State and Federal levels. In the last 10+ years, I've noticed that politics has gotten more extreme on both sides while the majority of the population sits somewhere in between and are more likely to be non-affiliated politically.

Culturally, I see a strong move towards populism in the US and abroad with right-leaning ideas and parties gaining ground despite media and corporate groups leaning more leftwards by the day.

My view is that the push by the media and corporations is more about money and attracting more consumer dollars and less about actually supporting what they appear to be supporting. My evidence is the lack of change in the demographics of their companies internally despite their overwhelming external support.

Due to the current trend of politicians on the left to move further left and further away from the ideas and beliefs of the majority of Americans as determined by polls, I see Trump winning a second term in 2020 with a confidence level of 85%.

Where There Is Life There Is Growth

If a state is growing in population, it is alive and thriving, but if its population is shrinking, then it's on a path towards decline. I monitor state migration trends because they let me know which states will experience job and business growth, house value appreciation and rental rate increase. I'll talk in detail about real estate later in this report.

I've reviewed a few studies from mortgage lender LendingTree, North American Movers and Atlas Movers. The summary of the studies is below.

Florida is the #1 destination. It was the top new destination for 15 of the 50 states. Considering it is a popular destination for retirees, this makes sense.

Texas had the highest number of people moving within the state based on mortgages. LendingTree showed that 93.4% of the mortgages were for mortgages somewhere else in the state.

South Carolina is top destination when adjusted for population size.

Tennessee made its second debut in the North American moving services Top 5 most inbound states in 2018. The state has also shown inbound migration every year since 2010 based on data from Atlas.

North Carolina has shown inbound migration in both North American and Atlas studies.

Overall the Southern States have had more inbound moves than some of the other regions. This includes Tennessee, Texas, Florida, Georgia, North Carolina and South Carolina.

Western states have had more overall inbound moves than the Midwest and Northeast. This includes Idaho which is the fastest-growing state according to North American Movers (most likely due to its low tax burden). Oregon, Arizona and Colorado have consistently been at the top among Western states for inbound migration.

The data suggests that there is a possible correlation between states with high property, income and other taxes and the outbound migration rate.

If the correlation in the data is correct, states like Florida, Tennessee and Texas should expect to see further growth.

North American Moving Services Migration Data

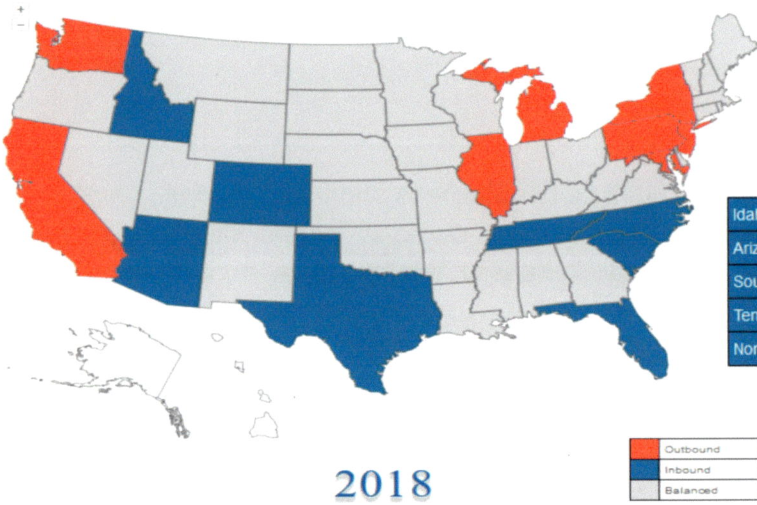

Top inbound states

State	%
Idaho	72%
Arizona	67%
South Carolina	63%
Tennessee	62%
North Carolina	61%

Top outbound states

State	%
Illinois	69%
California	64%
New Jersey	63%
Pennsylvania	61%
Maryland	58%

Atlas Migration Data

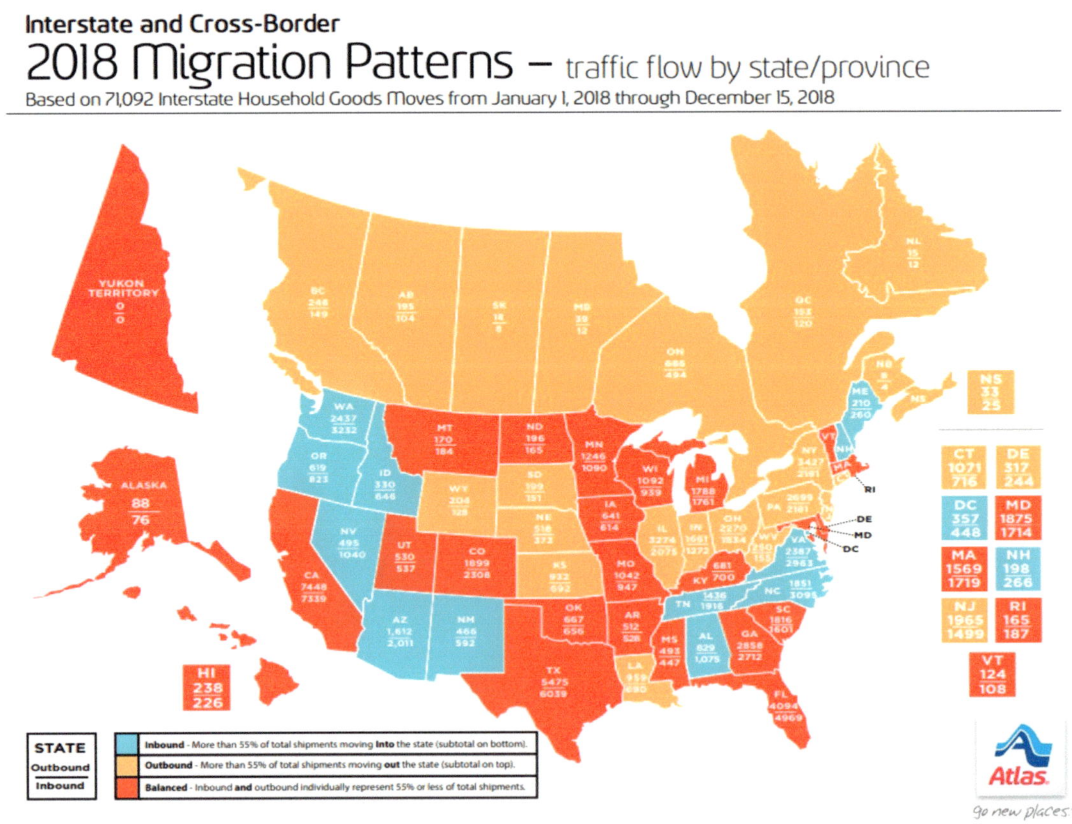

STATE Outbound Inbound	
(light blue)	**Inbound** - More than 55% of total shipments moving **Into** the state (subtotal on bottom).
(yellow)	**Outbound** - More than 55% of total shipments moving **out** the state (subtotal on top).
(red)	**Balanced** - Inbound **and** outbound individually represent 55% or less of total shipments.

Lending Tree Migration Data

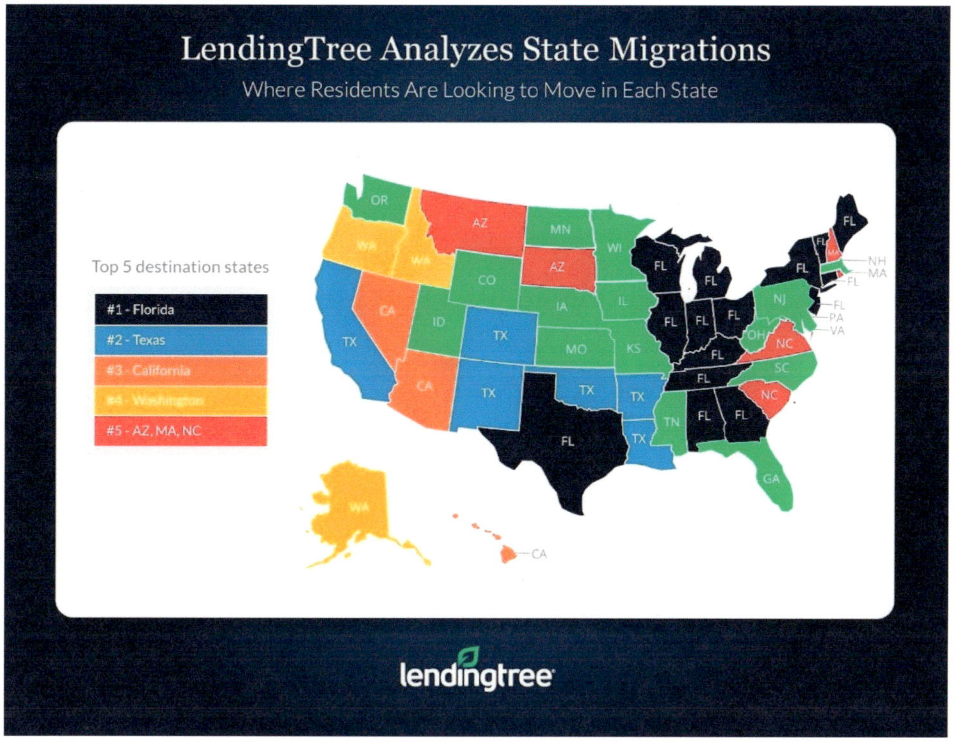

US Census Population Growth by County

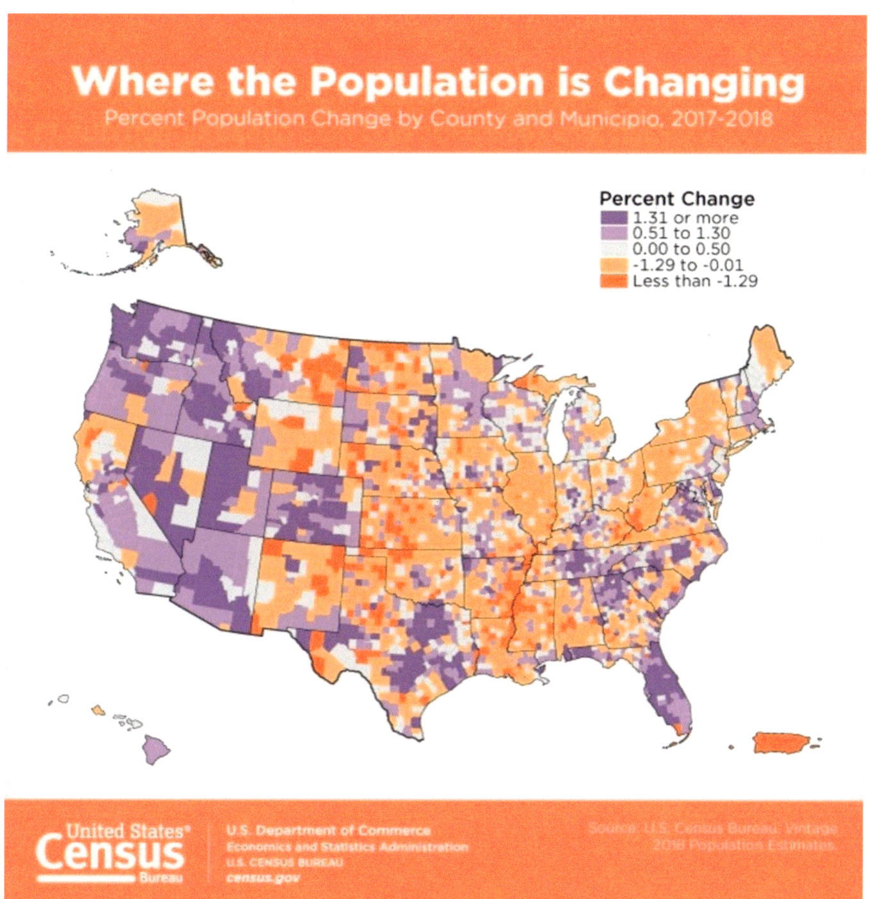

The shifts in migration trends should not be ignored when considering where you will live, work, build your business and invest.

The trends we are currently witnessing will most likely continue for decades to come due to them being driven by economics and demographics. To put it simply, money and people aging are driving these moves.

<u>"I'm No Longer Local, My Thoughts Are Global. That's Why I Seem Distant, Son Expand Your Vision"</u>

Here is what is on my mind when it comes to global growth…

By 2100, half of babies born worldwide are expected to be born in Africa

% of babies born, by region

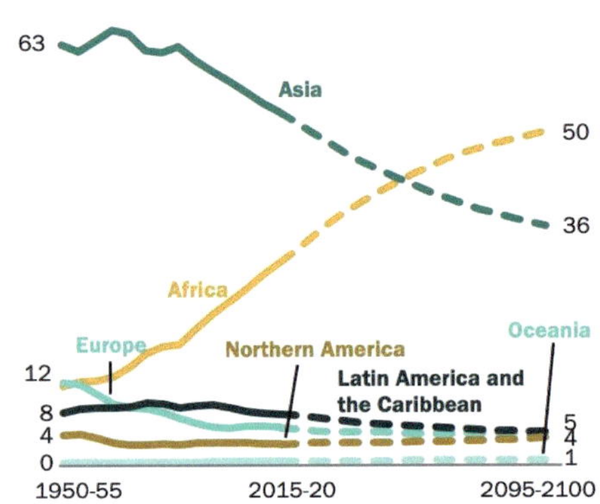

Note: Regions follow United Nations definitions and may differ from other Pew Research Center reports.
Source: United Nations Department of Economic and Social Affairs, Population Division, "World Population Prospects 2019."

PEW RESEARCH CENTER

AFRICA

Africa is projected to have the most babies born by about 2050, and they are currently the region with the youngest population.

Where there are births and young people there is innovation, health and growth.

Currently, China has the most births, but like Western countries, their population is quickly aging.

With aging populations, come the costs associated with aging like higher healthcare expenses and less consumption due to already having made most major life purchases like homes, cars, education, childcare etc.

An aging population world-wide is already starting to have effects in the US, Europe and Japan, where people 50+ of age are one of the fastest-growing worker demographics.

In Japan, they are already at the point where more Adult Diapers are being sold than Baby Diapers.

Countries that will be driving population growth will likely be driving economic and technological growth in the future.

We saw this with the growth of China as they shifted from an agriculture driven economy to a manufacturing and technology-driven economy.

This means that Africa may be on the path to become the breadbasket of the world due to the large amounts of land area which can be farmed.

The World's Oldest and Youngest Populations by Country

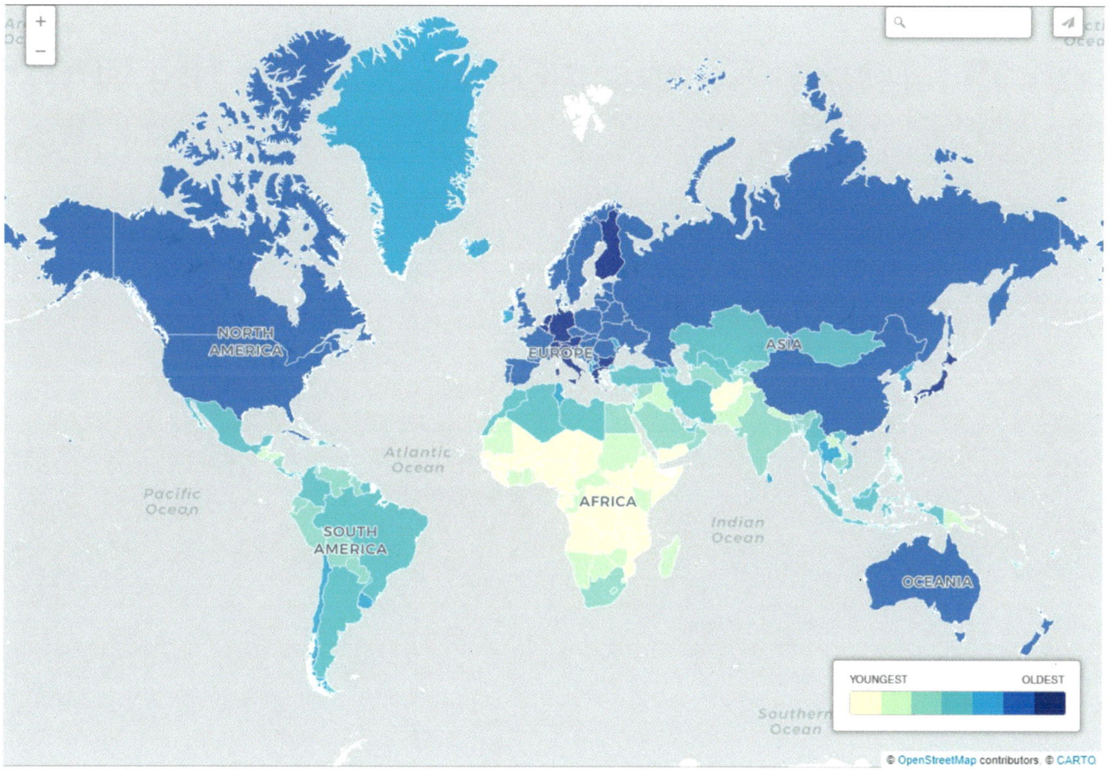

Fast Growing Economies in the World

7 of the 10 fastest growing economies in the world are in Africa.

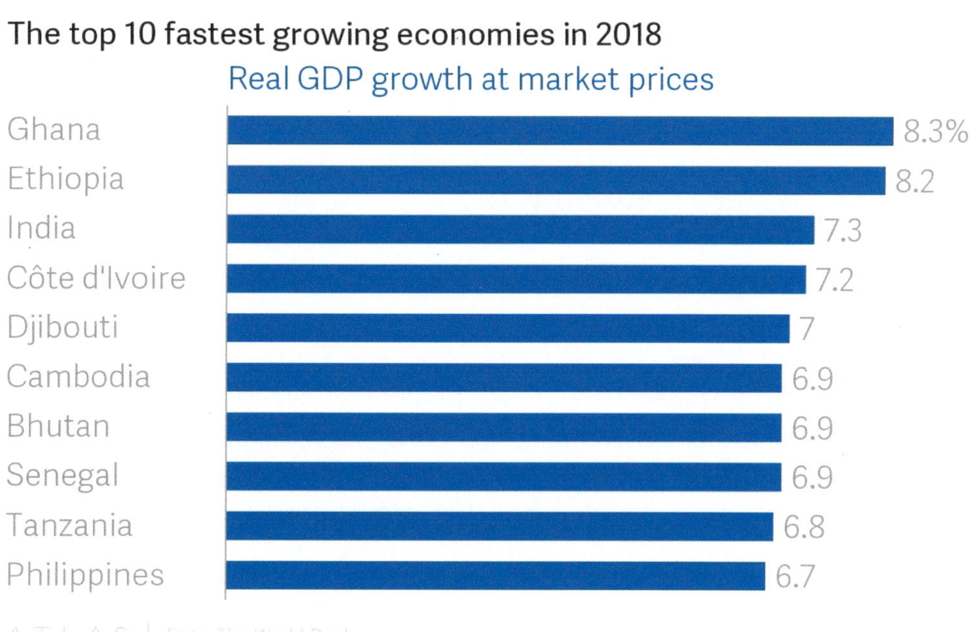

Projections for the Fastest Growing Economies in 2019 and 2023
In my view, these projections mark the beginning of trends that will last decades.

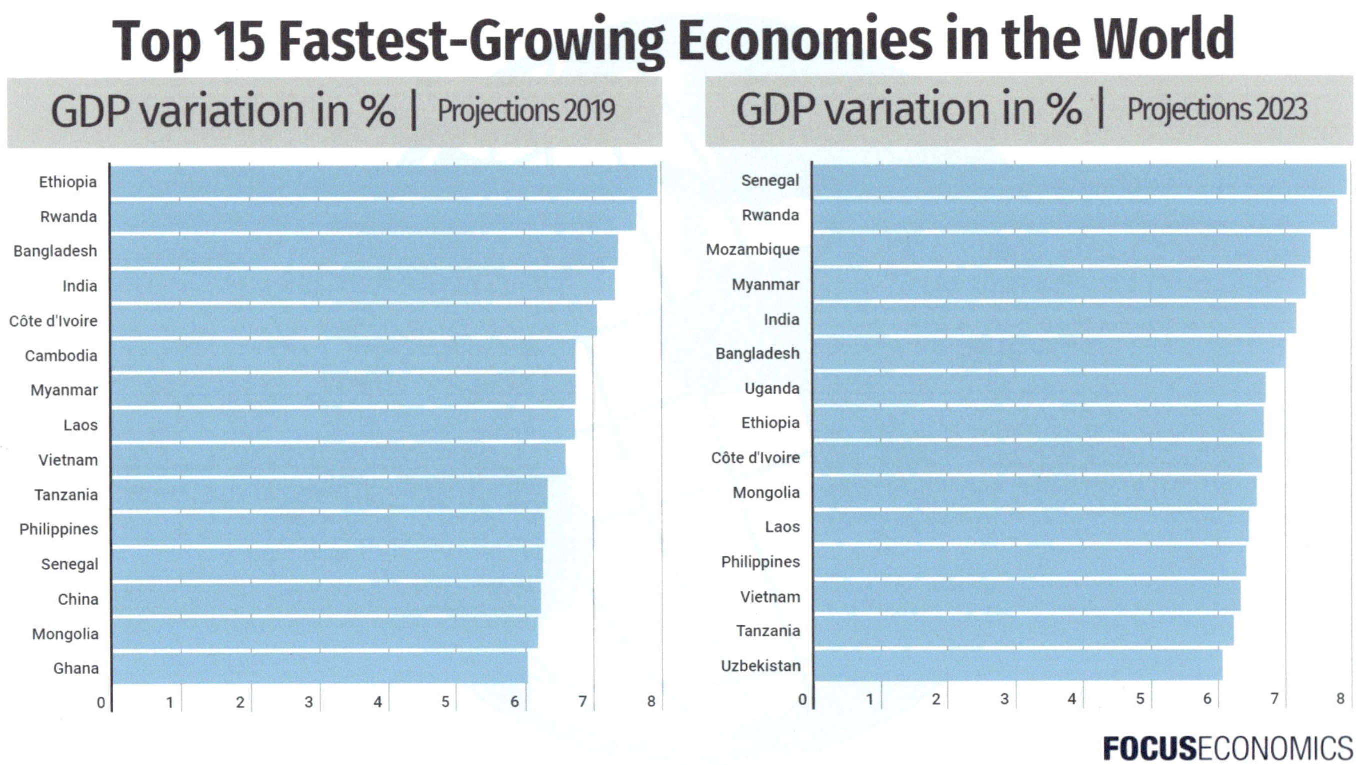

Demographics Are Destiny

We are currently going through the largest shift in demographic trends in human history. Both in the United States and the world. The coming wealth transfer will see trillions transferred from older generations to younger generations.

The global population of the "oldest old" — people aged 80 and older — is expected to more than triple between 2015 and 2050, growing from 126.5 million to 446.6 million. The oldest old population in some Asian and Latin American countries is predicted to quadruple by 2050.

Additionally, by 2050, global life expectancy at birth is projected to increase by almost eight years, climbing from 68.6 years in 2015 to 76.2 years in 2050

The same way that the Baby Boomers sparked the growth of global trends and brands due to the size of the group, their demographics will continue to shape our country and world. Baby Boomers, born 1944-1964 and age 55-75 in 2019, gave life to global brands like Pampers and Gerber when they were babies, sparked the largest auto purchase and housing boom in history when they grew families and are now reshaping healthcare as they grow older.

Millennials born 1981-1996 and age 23-38 in 2019, are now the largest working population and are driving the growth of trends like the Sharing Economy. An economy, where less value is placed on owning things and more value is placed on experiences. They are also changing trends in politics, investing, family creation, auto purchases and home-ownership.

While many companies have attempted to try to cater to Millennials, they have been mostly unsuccessful. This is because most companies that are used to dealing with other generations have ignored 3 things that weren't a common experience with the other generations 1) the amount of information available to Millennials, 2) greater options than were available to the previous generations and 3) the valuing of experiences over things.

This massive amount of debt doesn't show up a lot of places but does show up in the average net worth of the varying generations.

<u>Average and Median Net Worth for Various Generations</u>
Baby Boomers have an average net worth of $1,066,000 and a median net worth of $224,000.
Gen Xers' average net worth is around $288,700, but the median is $59,800.

Millennials have an average net worth of around $76,200, but their median net worth is only $11,100.
Gen Z's average net worth is difficult to report on since so much of the generation has no net worth or career.

The median net worth of Millennials, which means that half are above $11,100 and half are below that amount, does hint that there are many Millennials who have negative net worth due to debt. Also, the total amount of their assets is lower.

Generation Z, born 1965-1979 and age 40-54 in 2019, has the highest amount of debt, but the value of their assets helps offset their debt load.

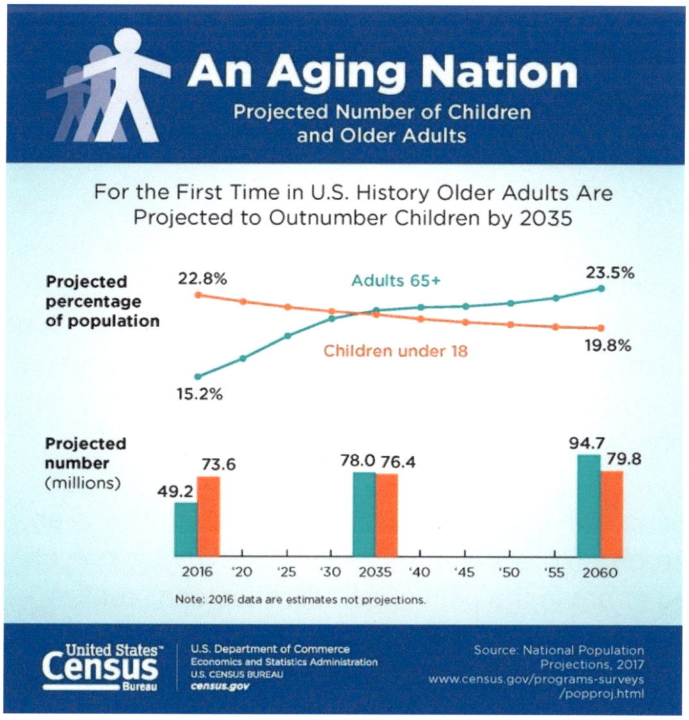

<u>The Greying of America</u>

By 2030, all Baby boomers will be over the age of 65 and 1 in 5 Americans will be of retirement age. By 2050, the population of people aged 65+ in America is expected to grow from around 50 million currently, to 88 million.

This means that there will be a great opportunity to provide technology, healthcare, housing and other products and services to this growing group. They not only will be growing but they will also be the wealthiest population in US history.

We will likely continue to see hospitals, urgent care facilities, active living communities, boutique senior housing, asset management, estate planning services and other areas grow.

I also see the aging of America drastically changing the housing market.

Home Is Where the Heart Is

As Baby Boomers retire and Gen Xers move closer to retirement by the year, I see them wanting to downsize from the large houses and McMansions they once lived in. I also see them wanting to be closer to modern conveniences like groceries, shopping and high-speed internet (you'd be shocked at how many people in suburban and rural communities have to rely on dialup and satellite internet).

I see things like golf courses and older suburban shopping malls declining dramatically. I also see nicer areas that are closer to cities and towns growing.

My expectations are for the amount of square footage in homes, apartments and per person to reverse trend and start decreasing.

I've recently been visiting various states looking at houses on the market and off the market. Talking to residential and commercial real estate brokers and real estate investors.

There seems to be a common theme. Lots of people can see the recent uptrend reversing course soon, but most don't know when that will happen.

I've researched this thoroughly on the ground, so here is my perspective.

My Hidden Housing Insight

My view is that the housing market has already started to turn in certain markets. I'll back this up with data soon enough.

I've driven thousands of miles and spent months researching this in NC, SC, VA, MD and DC. My aim is to be a real estate investor when people realize that the housing market is declining and it becomes a buyer's market.

Things I've noticed are as follows:

1. Most real estate investors in residential and commercial markets are over estimating their market's ability to afford the prices they are asking for rentals and housing. This applies to people with one property and people with 1,000+ units. There has been a trend towards luxury housing with high end everything. However, many aren't considering that wages haven't kept pace with housing costs over the last 20 years and that many markets and areas have a natural ceiling for how much people will pay to live in an area.

While driving around one day, it hit me that despite there being high home sales and rental rate comps in an area, at a certain price point, people will just live somewhere else (i.e. a better neighborhood). This is one of the problems that investors in areas that are being gentrified or are in the path of gentrification don't realize. While some buyers will take on the risk to own in an "up and coming area," most won't, especially if they have a family.

2. Most real estate investors and developers are also overestimating their market's desire to own single-family houses in the locations they are investing and building. This is based on my realization that most people under 40 could care less about the perceived "status" that comes with owning a home and are okay to rent if renting gives them more freedom and options, especially if they can rent in a nicer area with little investment

other than a security deposit. The other thing many investors are ignoring is that some areas and neighborhoods may always be perceived as working-class neighborhoods and not affluent due to their zip code, style of home, area etc. This subconscious perception is another factor that puts a ceiling on the maximum amount people are willing to spend on housing in an area.

However, you can still profit in any area if you buy smart and set the right expectations. Remember that the expected profit on any investment should be determined when you buy and not when you sell. This means controlling or purchasing real estate deals which, are a discount to their retail value.

Looking forward, I see a lot of value in owning real estate that cashflows much more than the expenses and debt service. If there is a housing downturn, calculate how your properties would perform if there were a 10% - 20% drop in monthly rental rates.

Zip codes that are trending towards recovery and gentrification may offer the best return on investment, but which have been affluent over decades will be the areas where people will always want to live. During economic downturns, affluent neighborhoods will also experience the least amount of real estate depreciation.

Next, you will get an analysis of one of my favorite real estate markets, Charlotte, NC. These methods can be applied to any market and I've applied them to markets all over the nation.

<u>Analyzing a Housing Market</u>

I started by finding out which months were the best and worst times to sell your house.

Month	% of Homes Selling Above List Price	Median Sales Price at Closing	Median Days on Market Before Closing
1. Jan	23%	$254,914	104
2. Feb	24%	$260,086	101
3. Oct	17%	$262,943	84
4. Nov	15%	$270,571	87
5. July	22%	$259,000	70
6. Dec	16%	$275,329	95
7. Mar	26%	$261,386	86
8. Sept	19%	$266,029	81
9. Aug	20%	$264,143	75
10. May	25%	$260,629	68
11. Apr	26%	$262,457	73
12. June	24%	$307,571	67

This table is based on a study of data from the Census Bureau, Realtor.com, Zillow and the Federal Reserve.

My goal as an investor is to buy when people are selling, which means I'm looking to buy at a discount and to sell when people are buying which means I can sell at a premium. This rule applies to any market I'm involved in.

Here is a look at several key metrics during May of each year, 2015-2019. May was chosen because it had the best balance of selling above list prices and days on the market before they were sold at closing.

I follow several housing market metrics that should show a slowing, sideways or declining growth rate. They are the following:

1. Closed Sales
2. Percent of Original List Price Received
3. Days between Listing and Closing
4. Days on the Market Until Sale
5. Cumulative Days on the Market Until Sale

Charlotte, NC Data

May of 2015-2019

Key Metrics	2015	2016	2017	2018	2019
New Listings	5,392	5,680	6,145	6,408	6,587
Pending Sales	4,123	4,477	4,849	4,797	5,627
Closed Sales	3,836	4,290	4,737	4,841	4,864
Median Sales Price	$200,000	$210,000	$223,750	$245,900	$259,900
Average Sales Price	$249,826	$257,940	$270,787	$299,723	$309,859
Percent of Original List Price Received	95.5%	97.%	97.%	98.%	97.3.%
List to Close	116	106	97	88	**88**
Days on Market Until Sale	67	54	46	39	**41**
Cumulative Days on Market Until Sale	81	63	54	46	**51**
Inventory of Homes for Sale	14,582	12,268	11,381	10,506	9,443
Months Supply of Inventory	4.4	3.4	2.9	2.6	2.3

Percent Change Year-Over-Year	2015	2016	2017	2018	2019
New Listings	-	+ 5.34%	+ 8.19%	+ 4.28%	+ 2.79%
Pending Sales	-	+ 8.59%	+ 8.31%	- 1.07%	+ 17.30%
Closed Sales	-	+ 11.84%	+ 10.42%	+ 2.20%	**+ 0.48%**
Median Sales Price	-	+ 5.00%	+ 6.55%	+ 9.90%	+ 5.69%
Average Sales Price	-	+ 3.25%	+ 4.98%	+ 10.69%	+ 3.38%
Percent of Original List Price Received	-	+ 1.36%	+ 0.52%	+ 0.21%	**- 0.21%**
List to Close	-	- 8.62%	- 8.49%	- 9.28%	**+ 0.00%**
Days on Market Until Sale	-	- 19.40%	- 14.81%	- 15.22%	**+ 5.13%**
Cumulative Days on Market Until Sale	-	- 22.22%	- 14.29%	- 14.81%	**+ 10.87%**
Inventory of Homes for Sale	-	- 15.87%	- 7.23%	- 7.69%	- 10.12%
Months Supply of Homes for Sale	-	- 22.73%	- 14.71%	- 10.34%	- 11.54%

To summarize what this data is saying.

- The number of Closed Sales is slowing at +0.48% vs +2.20% last year.
- The percentage of the asking price that sellers want is negative at -0.21%.
- The number of days that it takes for homes to be sold is stagnant at 0.0% instead of decreasing as it has in the past few years.
- The number of days that homes are on the market is up +5.13% vs being down -15.22% in 2018.
- The cumulative days that homes are on the Market Until Sale are up +10.87% versus being down 14.81% year-over-year in 2018.

When combined with the number of Price Increases versus Price Decreases, the data in the tables paint a clear picture of a housing market that is slowing in one of the most popular metropolitan areas in the nation.

This trend is the same in many markets across the United States and the world.

Chicago, New York, San Francisco, Dubai, London and Tokyo. Around the world housing prices are declining.

The information I'm about to tell you is to help prevent a world of heartache for you and your loved ones.

There Is Little To No Money in Owning a House That You Live In

To get back to basics, assets put money in your pocket every month. Liabilities take money out of your pocket.

Yes, people have bought houses and made money. But some have bought houses and lost money. Most people that made money have no idea how they made it and what factors contributed to their success. This is because they got lucky and benefited from one of the longest growth periods in history, which was powered by Baby Boomers earning and spending trillions. However, that luck streak has ended.

The only time you should by a house is to own it for 10+ years or as an investment property to generate cash flow for yourself. I say this because earning rent from a tenant that rents your entire home or from tenants that are renting bedrooms from you puts money in your pocket every month.

I also say this because we will see the death of many suburbs due to many people wanting to live closer to modern conveniences. As I mentioned before, the McMansions that plague the suburbs were built for time when people had larger families. Those times have changed so the factors that drove the appreciation of those areas have changed.

If you do decide to buy in a suburb, focus on the areas with the best school districts, lowest crime, modern conveniences, a growing population of younger people or affluent areas. People with families will always want to live in areas with good schools.

If you don't buy in the suburbs, safe areas that have a working-class population of people that may work in trades, retail, healthcare, hospitality etc. will provide a steady flow of tenants although the area may not see as much appreciation from existing property values.

Regardless of where you invest in housing, you should have an idea of who your future tenant or buyer would be. What they do for a living. How much they earn. How long they may stay. Where they are in terms of career and family creation. Also, people tend to live near and around other people who are most like themselves.

Also, if you do decide to go the home construction or development route, always do market research and account for lower than current market value on land, rents and neighborhoods, especially on spec (speculative) homes. These developments and homes may offer high returns, but also have the most risk if there is a national or regional housing downturn. This risk can be minimized using presales or by focusing on multifamily residential (2-4 units) or commercial (4+ units) development.

What Works Now May Not Work In The Future

This saying also applies to who works now.

There has been no better time in US history to learn and achieve the career or business that you desire. Thanks to the internet, certification classes, remote work and other tools, you can almost change careers or grow within a new field in just a few months.

While this technology has benefits, it also has costs. Costs such as it eliminating jobs permanently.

Technologies like Artificial Intelligence, Machine Learning, Robotics and Automation will drastically impact who even has a job in the future.

The one way that you and any business can stay ahead of the curve and ensure future income is by learning these technologies.

I spent years working in Artificial Intelligence and have used what I learned from witnessing that technology grow and takeover industries to forecast what other technologies will follow similar paths.

Areas that will see growth in the future:	These are fields that are perfect for disruption:
• Artificial Intelligence • Machine Learning • Nanotechnology • Wearable Technology • Home and Office Automation • Big Data Analysis • Data Recovery • Data Security • Robotics • Internet of Things • Fintech • Digitization and Tokenization	• Healthcare • Life Insurance • Property Insurance • Agriculture • Waste Management • Physical Asset Management • Trades • Legal Professions • Auto Sales • Logistics • Ecommerce • Financial Services

Riding Climate Cycles

No this isn't about some solar-powered bicycle. This is about how almost everything most people have been told about Climate Change has been a lie. Now, scientists are finally realizing the objective truth about the climate and how humans have virtually no influence or control over it as it relates to the Earths temperature.

First, Carbon and Carbon Dioxide are no more harmful to the planet than sunlight. The Greenhouse Effect is playground theories spread as facts with no way to prove or disprove it but pushed with the help of political and corporate agendas that are very profitable for their promoters.

However, what can be proven is that the Earth has gone through warming and cooling cycles throughout its entire existence.

This chart to the right shows how temperature has gone up and down over the last 10,000+ years.

Keep in mind that the Industrial Age didn't start until 1740. This is the age that started the mass production of Carbon Dioxide due to the burning of fossil fuels, wood and coal. As you can see several warming periods were much warmer than the most recent one, which most likely ended in 2000.

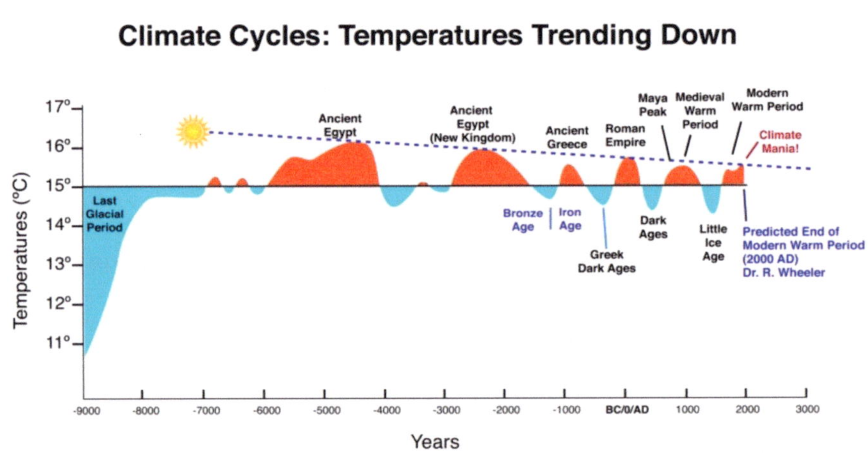

I say all of these words to say one thing…

Humans have no control over the temperature of the planet and whether seas rise or fall. We never have had control over this complex system and we never will. Don't let people try to control you by using guilt and shame to influence your decisions (they either want your votes, want you to spend money/pay more taxes or both).

Now, to talk about what really matters and has been proven: The Sun's influence on global temperatures.

Staring Into the Sun

The only factor that could influence Earth's climate, which also externally influences the climate of all of the planets in our solar system is the Sun. It is the only thing with enough energy to drive global changes in temperature. When combined with factors like Oceans, Polar Ice Caps, Volcanoes and our Atmosphere it becomes a lot clearer that an external influence impacts all of the Earth's interwoven systems.

The Sun, like the Earth, also has cycles called "Sunspot Cycles" that often last for 11 years. Sunspots are holes in the sun's surface.

During times when there are more sunspots, called "Solar Maximums", the temperature on earth is often higher. And during times when there are fewer sunspots, called "Solar Minimums" the temperature on the earth is often lower.

The correlation between higher and lower temperatures is shown in the following table that includes the prediction for Solar Cycle 25, which is expected to start in mid-2019 or 2020 and will peak between 2023 and 2026. That table shows the number of sunspots in red dots and blue lines and correlates that with the change in global temperatures as shown by the black line.

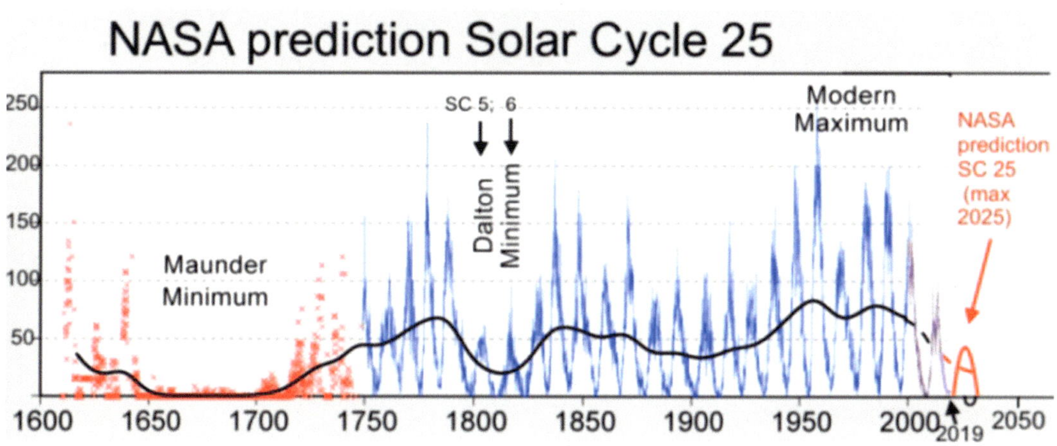

According to NASA, Solar Cycle 25 is projected to be the weakest cycle in the last 200 years.

There was a time in the past that had a similar amount of low solar activity over several solar cycles. It was called the Dalton Minimum.

The Dalton minimum lasted about 40 years from 1790-1830. This period of lower temperatures was made even cooler due to volcanic eruptions. This brings me to my next point.

Shake, Rattle and Solis

Solis is the Latin word for “Sun” and while that part is only slightly relevant, what is more relevant is that periods of low Sunspot activity have correlated with increased Global Earthquakes and Volcanic activity.

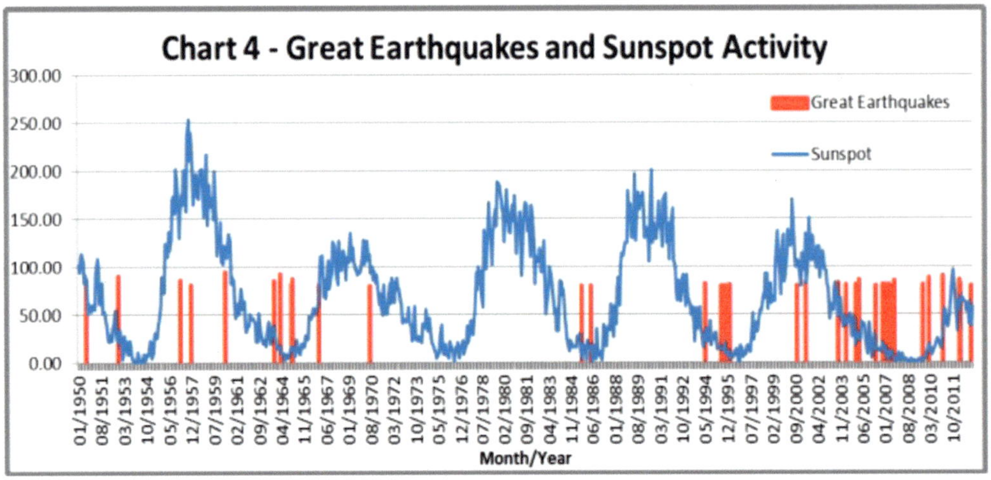

This first chart to the left shows the number of Great Earthquakes (Magnitude 7+) during various Solar Cycles.

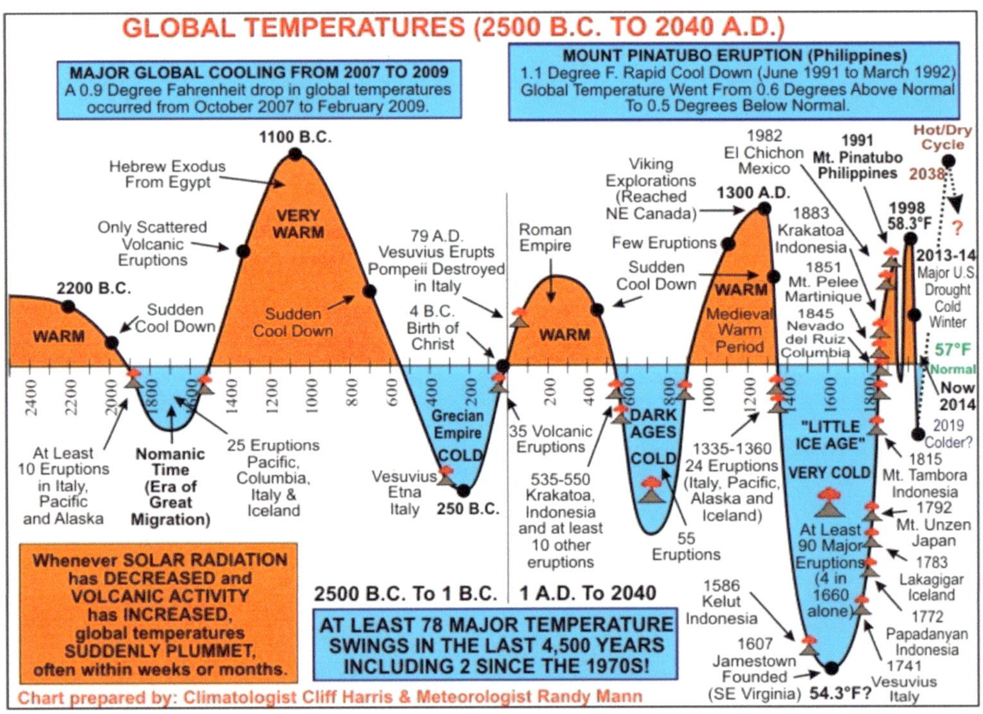

This second chart shows the occurrence of large volcanic eruptions overlapping with various cold periods throughout history.

Knowing that we may be going through a period of drastic climate changes is important when making decisions about where you will live, invest, grow your career and business.

Very few decisions in our lives, in business or the markets, are made without considering outside factors. So, use your awareness and intuition to estimate which areas people will want to live in and what will people need to buy if temperatures do turn colder. Ask what services will people, businesses, farmers and city, state and federal governments need.

One place where we may start to see the impact of shifts in climate are in farming and agriculture. If farmers are unable to grow crops and feed livestock, then this will directly impact local and national grocery stores, food supply chains and financial markets.

This is already happening with farmers reporting cool and wet weather that has led to flooded fields and wild weather swings with days of rain followed by a scorching heat.

Market Mindset

Financial markets have always been a passion of mine for decades. Even today, I still check US and Global market performance across asset classes.

This section will not give you specifics of what to buy or sell, but I can give you the information that will allow you to determine when market trends are changing, so you can arrive at your own conclusions.

The following chart shows the various phases of Market Cycles. With this chart, you can apply the information to whichever markets you want to invest in. My advice is to know your risk tolerance, your investment hold time and what the market will look like when you want to cash out your investment. No profit is real until it is realized and back in your bank account.

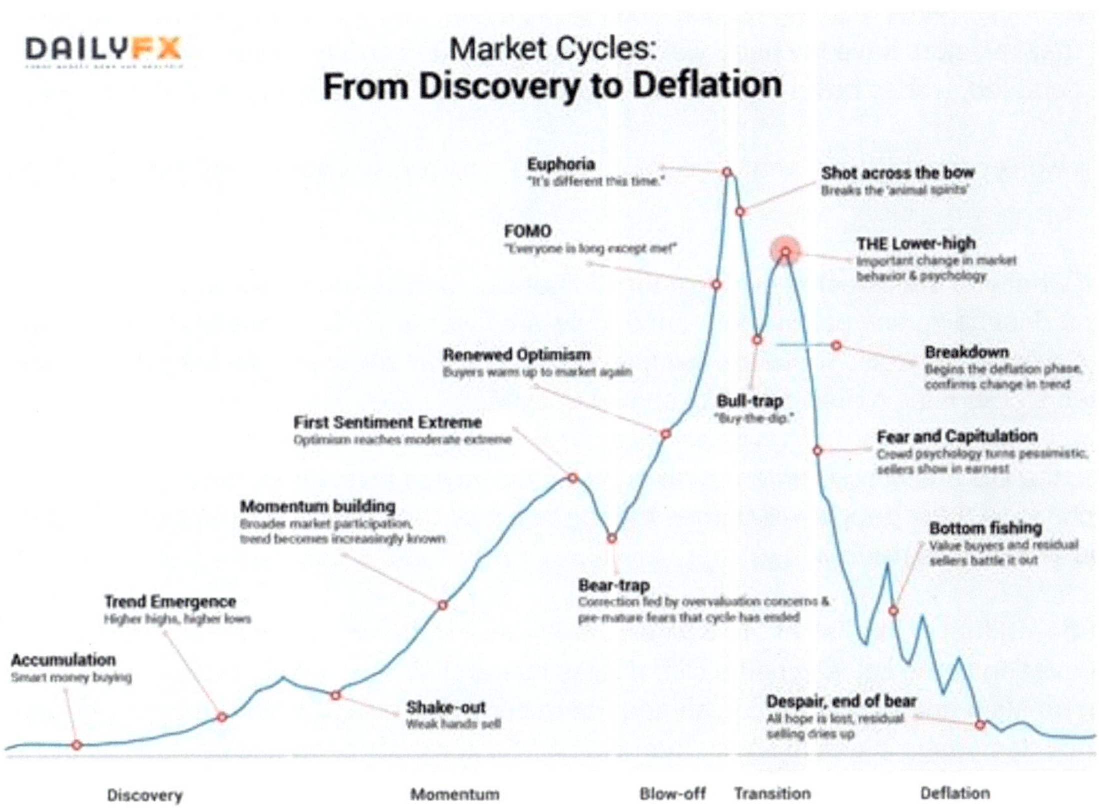

Fundamental and Technical analysis are topics for another day, but the key thing to remember when investing in financial and other markets are the following:

1. No markets go up forever.
2. It's never a bad thing to take a profit.
3. Assume your analysis is wrong and plan your exit strategy.
4. Profit is made based on the price you buy at so focus on paying a good price upfront.
5. Don't get emotionally attached to your investment.
6. When the facts change, change your opinion
7. Everything else may lie, but the price tells the truth. Ignore the hype and noise. Focus on what matters.

<u>Financial Markets</u>

In the US and International markets, we've seen new highs in equity markets. However, interest rates are trending lower (and sometimes negative) at the same time.

The demand for government debt indicates that people around the world may be looking for the safety that comes with government debt.

This flight to safety may also be indicated in the recent increase in the price of gold and Bitcoin.

If the global economy was going into a recession, these are all the signs one would expect to see. However, job growth and equity markets are still going strong.

My interpretation is that the markets and new jobs don't necessarily mean that the economy is as strong as being portrayed in the media, earning reports and other outlets. In today's world, stock buybacks and cheap money mean that investors have to chase yield that makes having cheap money worth it. Also, while many jobs are being created, wages haven't increased when adjusted for inflation in over 2 decades.

The signs of a weak economy and what I'd consider to be a bipolar economy, are mentioned in the next few sections.

Regardless of what you are invested in, know that if financial markets head lower, cash is always a valid investment and depending on your risk tolerance there are inverse ETFs, funds and Swaps that allow people to profit from declining markets. There are even inverse ETFs that allow people to profit from declining housing-related stocks if the housing market should decline.

Additionally, in the US and abroad, interest rates are at the lowest levels they have been at in years, so money is extremely cheap. A lot of people will borrow money because they can, but what can't be ignored is what will happen once rates start to rise again.

We got a glimpse of that in the Fall of 2018 when the Federal Reserve raised rates and mortgage applications and new and existing home sales fell off a cliff. If rates rise and money gets tight again, we can see asset prices decline on Main and Wall Street. I can see home price depreciation, down rounds in many startup valuations, price decreases in global equity markets and tighter job markets as companies minimize their capital expenditures.

Times when money is cheap, are great to acquire financing and capital that can be put to work if markets should turn. This funding will allow smart people and businesses to acquire assets at decreased valuations when things like delinquencies, defaults, bankruptcies, cash flow issues, forced sales and takeovers start increasing as money gets tighter.

A focus on assets that generate net positive cash flow will be key to future success.

During times when money gets expensive, valuations become relative to the price someone is willing to pay for an asset. This means that with value being relative isn't as reliable when that money isn't exchanged as frequently during buy/sell transactions. However, cash flow is real and can be measured objectively.

Autos and Transportation

This section is mostly charts that aim to do two things 1) show you how the auto market isn't doing too well and 2) help you use your own perception to determine how to adapt to these trends.

The chart on the left looks at Class-8 truck sales, which are the trucks that are delivered to trucking companies and truckers. This shows that the number of truck sales is reaching a new peak.

However, the chart on the right below is showing that the number of Class-8 Truck Orders is plunging back to levels not seen since the last Transportation Recession that spanned mid-2015 to late 2016.

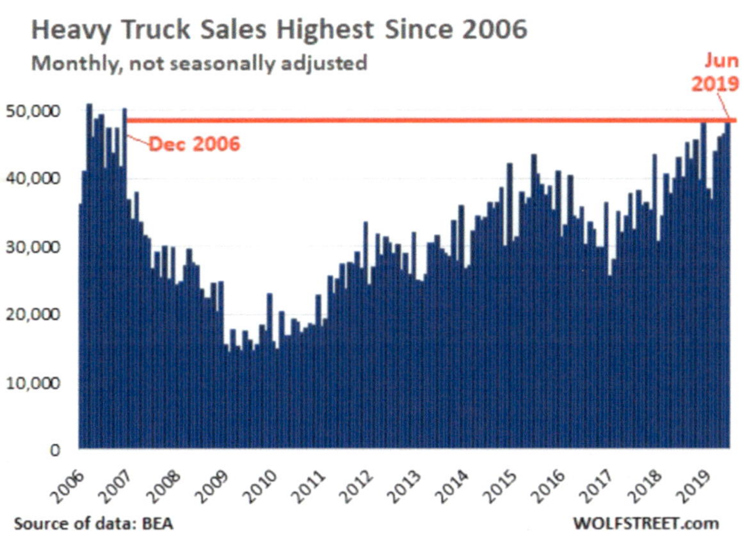

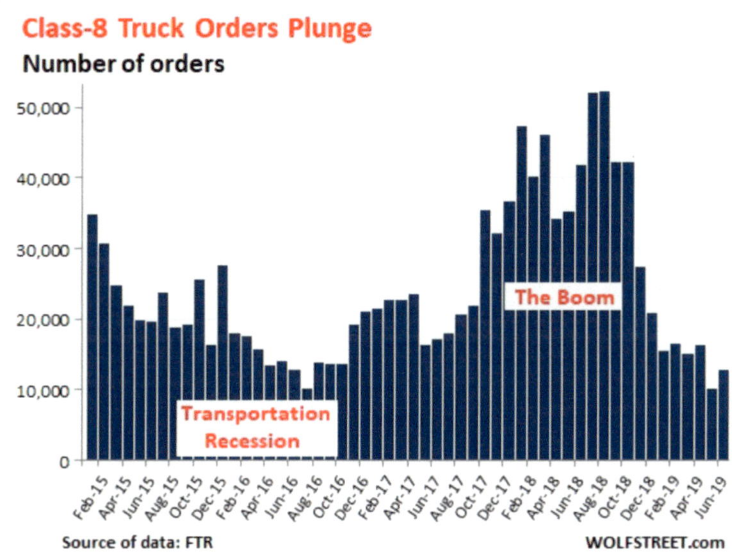

Below we have a chart of the new Passenger Car Registrations in the US. This data includes new private cars and commercial vehicles registered to authorities like mayors, postal workers, Federal employees etc.

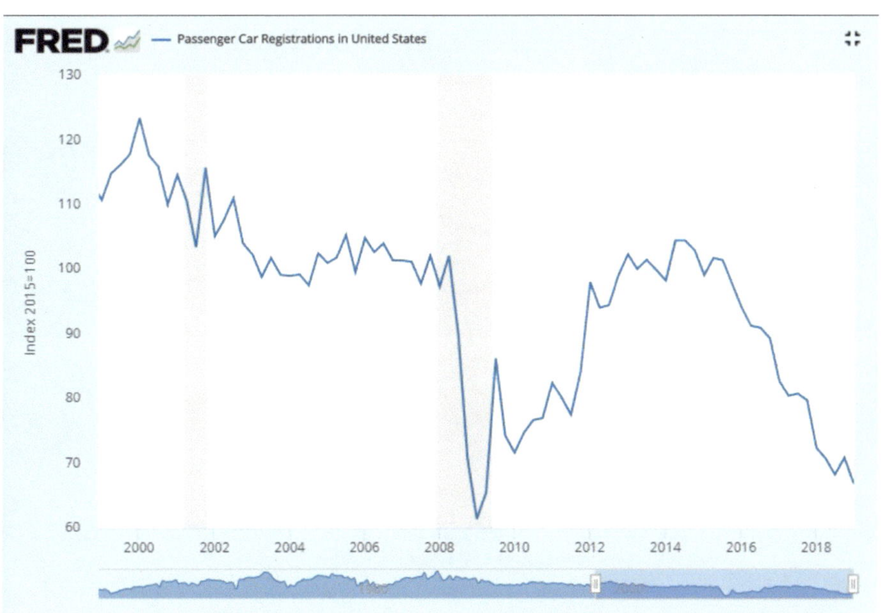

This chart indicates that Car Registrations are not only down but are approaching levels not seen since 2008 during the Global Financial Crisis.

While the data is open to interpretation, it does not indicate a healthy market for cars, car dealers, car lenders and related markets

The chart on the left below shows that New Car Sales are also down to levels not seen since 1999. This is despite having 20 years of population growth in the US since then.

The chart on the right below shows New Car Sales vs Used Car Sales. In both charts, you can see that New Car sales are declining. One thing that is also worth noticing is that the growth of Used Car Sales is slowing.

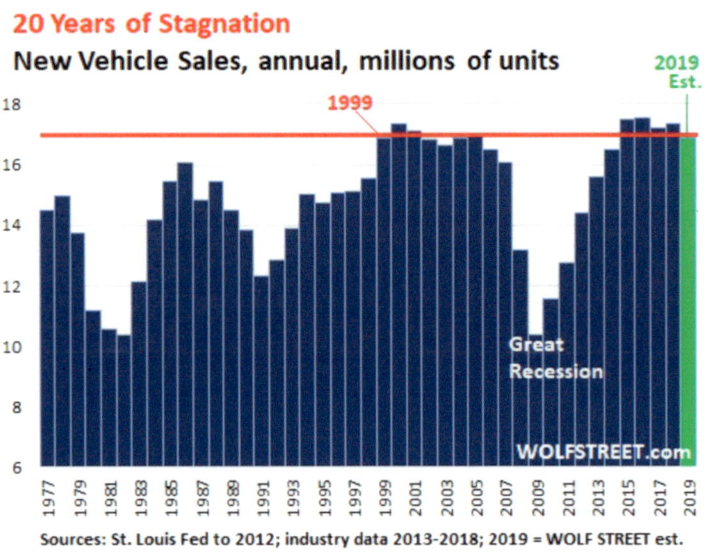

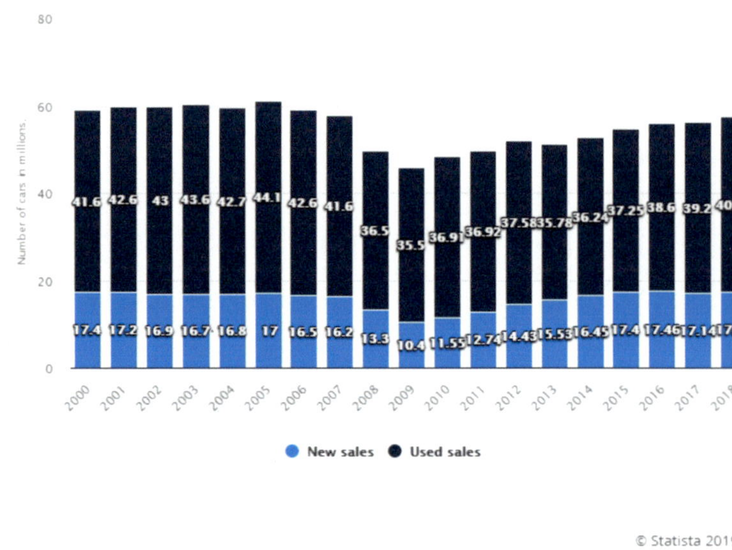

This is something to keep in mind if you're considering buying a car or if your profession is related to the auto industry.

Another factor that can't be ignored is auto loan delinquency rates. Around 7 million people are 90+ days delinquent on their auto loans. And that number is trending higher.

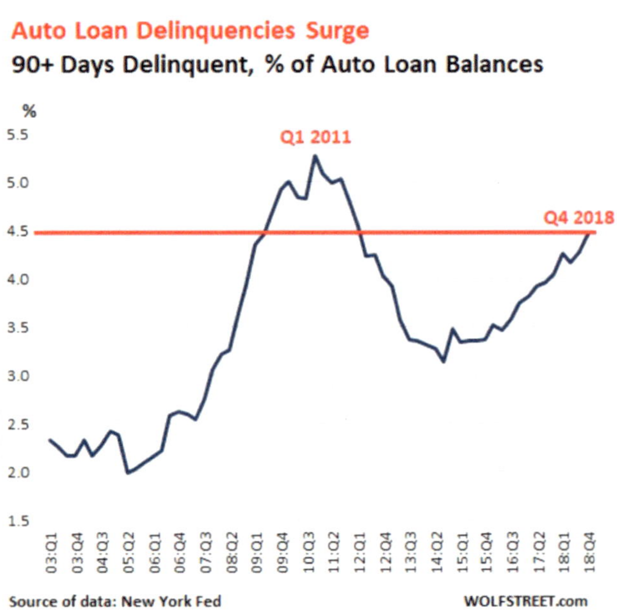

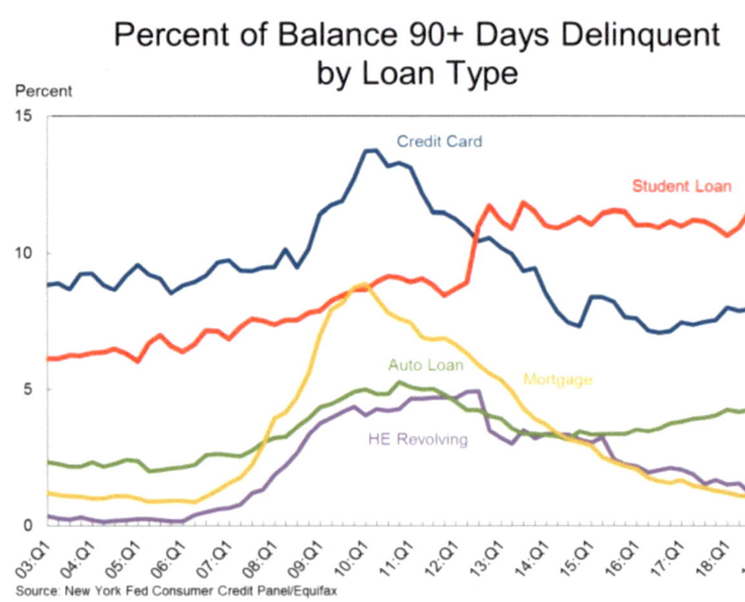

Finally, there is the Cass Freight Index which looks at all modes of domestic freight shipping and freight expenditures. The data indicates that shipments are down while expenditures spending on freight is up versus previous years. Although expenditures looks to be trending lower in 2019 compared to 2018.

This slowing in expenditures matches perfectly with the previously cited data that showed the slowing of Class-8 Truck Orders.

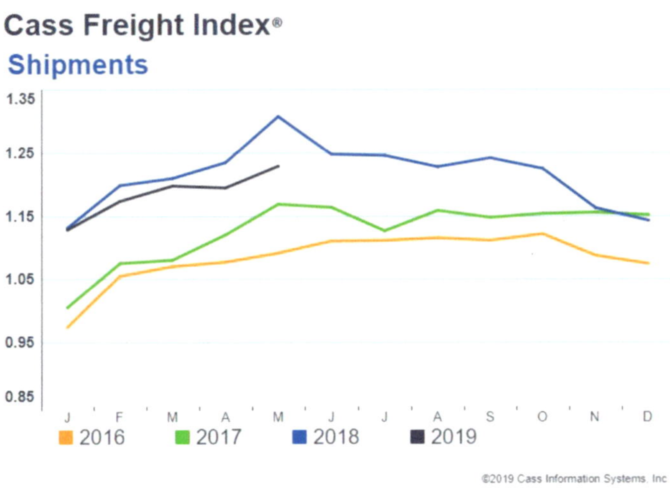

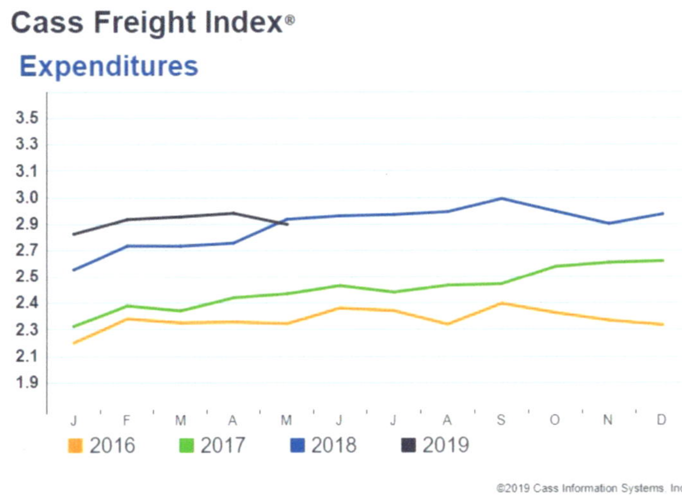

Appendix

Best Fields to Go Into That Don't Require a Degree Based On Earnings

General Contractor	Wind/Solar Energy Technician
Construction Manager	Oil and Gas Worker
Electrician	Commercial Diver
Plumbers	Web Developer
HVAC Technicians	Copywriter
Licensed Practical Nurse	Social Media Manager
Home Inspector	Video Editor
Energy Auditors	Graphic Designer
Environmental Scientist	User Experience/User Interface Designer
Civil Engineering Technician	Computer Programmer
Technical Sales	App Developer
Construction Equipment Operator	Data Recovery Specialist
Carpenter/Handyman	Telecommunications System Technician
Diesel Technician	Boilermaker
Automotive Mechanic	Brick Mason
Tractor Trailer Driver	Business/Industrial Automation
Medical Equipment Repair	Industrial Tool Programmer
Aviation Maintenance Technician/Mechanic	Logistics Manager
Heavy Equipment Mechanic	Dental Hygienist
Welder	Medical Technologist
Industrial Machinery Mechanic	Physical/Occupational Therapist
Software Tester	Radiation Technologist/Therapist
Insurance Adjuster	

Architectural or Civil Drafter Esthetician Career Coaching/Counseling	Diagnostic Medical Sonographer Elevator Installer/Repairer Phlebotomist Credit Counseling

Best Degrees to Acquire Based On Earnings

Petroleum Engineering Actuarial Mathematics Nuclear Engineering Chemical Engineering Electronics Engineering Communication Engineering Computer Engineering Aerospace Engineer Electrical Engineer Material Science and Engineering Biomedical Architectural Engineer Aviation Management	Physicist Statistician Mechanical Engineer Software Engineer Business and Information Technology Economist Industrial Engineer Applied Mathematician Civil Engineer Mathematician Computer Information Systems Manager Biotechnologist Construction Management

Best Certificates/Licenses To Acquire Based On Earnings

CompTIA Security+ CompTIA A+ AWS Cloud Practitioner AWS Big Data AWS Solutions Architect Google Cloud Certified Google Developer Certification Google Mobile Web Specialist Google Associate Cloud Engineer Google Cloud Certified - Professional Data Engineer Google Cloud Certified - Professional Cloud Architect Google Analytics Individual Qualifications Microsoft Technology Associate Microsoft Office Specialist (MOS)	Cisco CCNA Certified Construction Manager (CCM) Certified Financial Planner (CFP) Chartered Financial Analyst (CFA) Certified Public Accountant (CPA) Certified Scrum Master Project Management Professional Council Certified Ethical Hacker (CEH) Certified Information Systems Security Professional (CISSP) Certified Information Security Manager (CISM) Certified Information Systems Auditor (CISA) Certified Cloud Security Professional (CCSP) GIAC Security Essentials Certification (GSEC)

List of High Quality Coding Bootcamps	List of Online Certification/Course Resources
Lambda School General Assembly Bloc Thinkful Flatiron School The Tech Academy Hack Reactor Tech Talent South Epicodus	EdX Udemy Coursera Khan Academy

5 Figure Part-Time Careers (6 Figure if taken seriously)
Sales
Real Estate Agent
Copywriting
Editing
Virtual Assistant
Affiliate Marketing

6 Figure Paths (7 Figure if taken seriously)
General Consulting
Technical Sales
Pharmaceutical Sales
Internet Marketing
Franchise Owner
Insurance Adjuster
Short Term Rental Property Management

7+ Figure Paths

Securities Brokerage	Foreign Currency Exchange
Corporate Internet Marketing	Licensed Cryptocurrency Exchange
Executive/Management/Finance/Technical	Ecommerce Private Labeling
Recruiting Agency	Product Development
Licensed Drone Piloting	Real Estate Development
Real Estate Investing	Intellectual Property Licensing
Insurance Underwriters	B2B Technical Sales
Niche-Specific Consulting	Waste Management
Management Consulting	Supply Chain/Logistics Management
Marketing Agency	Residential/Commercial General Contracting
Investment Banking	Commercial Real Estate Property Management
Venture Capitalist	Fintech/AI/Blockchain/Platform Software/Web/App Development
Business Advisory	HIPAA/FinCEN/PCI Compliant Software Developer
Financial Asset Management	KYC/AML/CDD Service/Product Provider
Equity Market Trader/Investor	Federal/State Government Contracting
Registered Money Service Business (MSB)	

Congratulations!

You've reached the end of the **Profit From Possibilities** report.

Make sure you keep this report somewhere safe so you can reference it again over the years.

Also, send me any comments or feedback you may have or requests to retain my services.

And share what you've learned with your associates and loved ones so they can profit too.

Adrian Kennedy
Adrian.Kennedy@xscapeco.com

Made in the USA
Monee, IL
12 September 2026

62979097R00019